MY LITTLE GOLDEN BOOK ABOUT
VIKINGS

BY ANDY STJERN ♦ ILLUSTRATED BY MATT KAUFENBERG

A GOLDEN BOOK • NEW YORK

Text copyright © 2024 by Andy Stjern
Cover and interior illustrations copyright © 2024 by Matt Kaufenberg
All rights reserved. Published in the United States by Golden Books, an imprint of
Random House Children's Books, a division of Penguin Random House LLC, 1745 Broadway,
New York, NY 10019. Golden Books, A Golden Book, A Little Golden Book, the G colophon,
and the distinctive gold spine are registered trademarks of Penguin Random House LLC.
rhcbooks.com
Educators and librarians, for a variety of teaching tools, visit us at RHTeachersLibrarians.com
Library of Congress Control Number: 2023938875
ISBN 978-0-593-70330-4 (trade) — ISBN 978-0-593-70331-1 (ebook)
Printed in the United States of America
10 9 8 7 6 5 4 3 2 1

About 1,200 years ago, there lived a group of fearless warriors and sailors known as Vikings. Their home was in Scandinavia, an area of northern Europe that today includes Norway, Denmark, and Sweden. Here, the summers are short, and the winters are long and cold.

In the spring and summer months, after the ocean ice melted, the Vikings would leave home and sail to search for riches in foreign lands.

Because they relied on boats, Vikings became excellent shipbuilders. Their most famous boat was the longship. Longships came in different sizes, but the biggest ones measured up to seventy-five feet in length!

Vikings rowed their longships with long oars. Or a sail could be raised on windy days to increase speed and give the rowers time to rest. The longships were often decorated with colorful shields and sails, as well as large dragon heads on the front of the boat. These were thought to scare their enemies.

Sometimes, the Vikings traveled to get things they needed from people in other lands. They would bring their wool, fish, and ivory to trade. And they would get spices, fabric, and pottery in return.

But not all trips were friendly. Vikings were famous for raiding towns and villages to steal gold, weapons, and even people! They would bring these people back home to the Viking settlements and make them work.

Some of the most famous Vikings were unfriendly.

Erik the Red was living in Iceland when he was forced to leave after a bad fight with his neighbor. He sailed away in search of a new home and is thought to be the first Viking to reach Greenland.

Erik's son Leif Erikson grew up living in Greenland. An explorer himself, Leif and a crew of Vikings sailed more than two thousand miles and landed in North America—almost five hundred years before Christopher Columbus! The Vikings briefly settled in what is now eastern Canada. Leif called the area Vinland.

Ragnar Lothbrok was one of the first Vikings to invade England. He was famous for always attacking smaller armies than his own. Having more warriors on his side increased his chances of winning a battle.

Viking women took care of their homes, farms, and families while their husbands were gone for months or even years at a time. The strongest trained as warriors and went into battle with the men. These women were called shield-maidens.

One of the most famous shield-maidens was named Freydís. She was the daughter of Erik the Red and was part of the group that made it to North America. While there, Freydís scared off a band of attackers after the other Vikings ran away.

Lagertha, the first wife of Ragnar Lothbrok, would bravely race into battle and fight all enemies. Legend says Ragnar asked Lagertha to marry him because he was so impressed by her courage and strength.

Vikings didn't only have longboats—they also had longhouses! Longhouses made with wood were common in Denmark, Sweden, and Norway, where there were big forests with lots of trees to build with. A more simple turf house was common in Iceland, where there were fewer trees but a lot of grass.

Most longhouses had only one room—and families had their farm animals live inside with them during the winter! In the center of the house there was usually a fire pit for cooking meals and providing light and heat. A hole was cut in the roof above the fire so smoke could escape. Against the walls were wooden benches to sleep and sit on.

Vikings often built villages near the ocean or other bodies of water such as lakes and rivers. They were expert fishermen. They would catch trout, herring, and cod, and then preserve the fish so it could be stored and eaten during the long winters.

Farming was another way the Vikings got food. They grew wheat, oats, cabbage, peas, and other crops. In the summer months, apples, cherries, and plums were harvested from trees.

Vikings raised sheep, cows, pigs, and chickens. The animals provided food in the form of meat and eggs. And the fur, leather, and wool were used to make clothes.

The Vikings ate two meals a day: dagmal (day meal) and nattmal (night meal). Children would eat porridge for their day meal, perhaps with fruit and honey added. Adults would eat leftover stew with flatbread.

Stew was a common meal because it could be made in big pots and reheated and eaten for many days. The night meal would be more stew, possibly with fresh meat or bread.

Special occasions such as weddings, funerals, and the beginning of spring were celebrated with big feasts. Feasts offered a variety of good things to eat and drink. Plus, there was music, dancing, and games. A Viking feast could last many days!

Viking children did a lot of chores. Girls took care of the farm animals, tended the vegetable garden, cooked meals, and made clothing. Boys were responsible for hunting, fishing, collecting firewood, and fixing tools.

Doing all this hard work helped Viking children learn many valuable skills, such as how to ride a horse, start a fire, and sail a boat.

After work was done, there was time to play. Viking boys and girls had simple handmade toys like wooden swords, dolls, and boats.

The Vikings worshipped many gods and goddesses and often prayed to them for good weather or victory in battle.

Odin was the head god, known for his love of wisdom. Odin's son Thor was known as the god of thunder and the defender of all gods and goddesses. He carried a mighty hammer to use in battle.

Freya was the powerful goddess of war, love, and beauty. And Loki, the god of mischief, was known for being a trickster. He had the ability to shape-shift and pretend to be other people.

The greatest honor for a Viking was to die in battle with his sword or axe in hand. If a warrior had lived a noble and honest life, upon their death, they would be picked up by a Valkyrie—a Viking angel who rides a horse—and taken to Viking heaven called Valhalla.

The Vikings lived a long time ago, but they are still part of our lives today. You can see them in books, TV shows, and movies. Some days of the week are named after Viking gods—Thursday comes from Thor's Day. And Vikings are believed to have invented the hair comb. They carved them out of animal bones and antlers!

What do you think about the Vikings? Would you have liked to live the life of a Viking?